A Beginner's Guide to Disaster Survival

Food Procurement

Finding the Best Animal Food Sources

Prepping and Survival Books

Dueep Jyot Singh

Mendon Cottage Books

Mendon Cottage Books

JD-Biz Publishing

Download Free Books!

http://MendonCottageBooks.com

Disclaimer

The information is this book is provided for informational purposes only. It is not intended to be used and medical advice or a substitute for proper medical treatment by a qualified health care provider. The information is believed to be accurate as presented based on research by the author.

The contents have not been evaluated by the U.S. Food and Drug Administration or any other Government or Health Organization and the contents in this book are not to be used to treat cure or prevent disease.

The author or publisher is not responsible for the use or safety of any diet, procedure or treatment mentioned in this book. The author or publisher is not responsible for errors or omissions that may exist.

Warning

The Book is for informational purposes only and before taking on any diet, treatment or medical procedure, it is recommended to consult with your primary health care provider.

Our books are available at

1. Amazon.com
2. Barnes and Noble
3. Itunes
4. Kobo
5. Smashwords
6. Google Play Books

Table of Contents

Introduction

Survival, – especially in adverse conditions, when you have suddenly been faced with natural or man-made disaster, – is based on a particular mindset. You may have read about people who have managed to get through and survive disaster and catastrophes, which are potentially life-threatening. On the other hand, there have been people who went through extensive survival training, and still could not manage to use their particular skills effectively and beneficiary in order to survive.

So, even though the latter had the requisite knowledge and skills, what made them fail, when other lesser trained people succeeded? That is the will to survive.

I know about an Army officer who brought his group of seven men through an enemy ridden territory after 31 days of harrowing mental, physical and psychological trauma. It was not his army training, which brought him and his responsibility back to base safely. It was also not their knowledge, about how to get food, save themselves from the enemy, make fire, make or take shelter in the best place available, and other factors which could make all the difference between life and death.

The answer was mental attitude. He said that his men had complete faith in him. His men also knew that if the captain said "we cannot," they would not be able to reach in their goal. This trust and responsibility was one of the reasons why he did his best to achieve safety, even though many times his body and mind just said "you are being stupid, you cannot survive, just give up."

Now this man had a red-hot will to survive. His mind had begun playing him tricks, when the going got rough. It is going to happen to you also. It is so easy to say, I cannot do it, I do not have the power to do it. That is the coward's way out. Unfortunately, 98% of us are cowards. We are not going to make the effort, because, what is the use.

The rest 2% who say, I am not done, I will survive may be rare, but they are the leaders, they are the ones who have the willpower to motivate you to do your best, especially when you are inclined to moan or complain.

All your survival skills and training are going to come to naught, and are not going to serve any useful purpose, if you do not have this will to quit yourself against adverse conditions and survive.

All the training in the world cannot teach a person the will to survive.
You either have it or you do not.

Take Scarlett O'Hara as a guide – I will never go hungry again. She could so easily have said, well, Tara has burned down, so I will just place one hand over the other and sit down in a corner, and dream of past glory. It is so easy to do that. On the other hand, it is so difficult to get moving in a positive and practical manner, in order to survive. She took up the challenge. She survived.

I am certain a number of her detractors, who were extremely lazy, and could not be bothered to pick up the threads of their lives again must have considered her to be very unladylike. They would rather whine and moan and remain parasites on the face of the earth until the day they departed – unlamented and failures to the last. Because they were too lazy to adapt to changed circumstances and did not want to face reality.

The reality in this book may be hard to take by people who cannot imagine other people eating foodstuffs which they have been brought up to consider as inedible. In the East, ancient tradition says that anything which flew, walked, crawled and swam was good to eat. If you knew how to prepare it properly. And if you knew which portions of it to avoid so that you did not suffer from stomachache.

When you are face to face with catastrophe, the first thing you have to persuade your mind is to face reality. You are in a drastic survival environment. Your mind is going to be stressed out. What happened? This is the first impact upon your mind while he tries to deal with what it is facing at the moment. And then it tries to be practical. How hurt am I? What is the condition of the environment around me? And how am I to survive?

This book has tips and techniques in order to survive, along with humorous, psychological and practical stories and real-life episodes about the will to survive and the necessity of clear thinking. As well as other tall tales. So read on…

The Psychological Aspects of Leadership

There can only be one acknowledged leader in a group – he is going to be experienced, clear minded, and capable of making logical and beneficial decisions for the good of the group.

The ability of coping with these emotions, thoughts and feelings in that one particular instance of disaster and after it is what is going to make all the difference between success and failure. A well-trained and knowledgeable person can change into an ineffective, shock ridden and indecisive person in the blink of an eye, if his mind is not capable of surviving through the stress of change.

That is why, you as a potential victim of disaster and catastrophic situations and circumstances – man-made or natural – need to remember this fact. You are going to be stressed out, the moment you get past the first shock of disaster.

How easily you bounce back from that stressed-out situation is going to make the difference between life and death in the immediate present. Many people are so dazed, that they are on capable of logical and sensible thought. The rest of the family members need to take care of them because they are incapable of making decisions for themselves. If every member of the family is in that state of shock and indecisiveness, you are already beaten at stage one itself.

Many of us are definitely not going to face such a situation in our lifetime. On the other hand, the chances of us facing such a situation are growing larger every day, because of potential man-made and natural disasters like war, drought, floods and cyclones.

We may also find ourselves breaking down in the middle of the desert, because we forgot to fill our gas tank full of gas. Man's stupidity is Legion, and so is his carelessness. In fact, many idiotic escapist novelists use this theme with the stupid heroine going out in the snow, and getting lost. Of course, there is an equally moronic hero somewhere around snowbound in the wilderness on whose doorstep, she is going to wind up, and thus pass the winter in safe seclusion.

Did I add that this dimwit went out in the snow, without adequate maps, food, clothes, cell phone and a GPS system and if you are reading a Harlequin Desire or Blaze book, she is also going to be expecting a baby. How else are you going to sympathize with this stupid, single parent would-be mom in an interesting condition?

So naturally, she has to go out in the snow. After all she needs a father for her kid. The kid's original father skipped town, because he did not want the responsibility of a moron and baby around his neck. The hero is going to be somewhere around to save her, in the mountains. He has to be a multibillionaire. Or he has to be royalty or European aristocracy, spending a harsh winter in the mountain vastness in a broken down log cabin instead of in a warm chalet in the South of France. Also, he has to be unmarried. He has to be a cynic, who is going to fall for her and for her baby.

The baby is, of course, going to be delivered safe and sound, without any medical assistance, by these two amateurs. He is also going to have plenty of baby food and medicines in his one room cabin retreat to take care of both of them. And he is going to marry the nitwit on page 186, and take her back home to Moronia.

Talk about ridiculous submission guidelines. Escapist fiction caters to low level IQs, where you leave your credulity and reality at the doorstep.

In real life, such a moron is going to drive off the cliff because of low visibility and thus stop boring us with a predictable story plot. Or, the door is going to open and lo and behold, the hero's wife or partner is going to be standing there, with her arms akimbo, glaring at such a nitwit and giving her the opinion of such fluffy headed females who have no instinct of self-preservation. Going out in the snow and in such a condition, forsooth.

But then we bought the book, didn't we, because the blurb talked about TDH and beautiful mom and baby makes three.

Real life is definitely never like escapist fiction. We are not going to find heroes with welcoming doorsteps, saying, "Come in, come in, you can stay here, welcome, welcome, the kitchen and my bedroom are all yours, I will sleep on the bear rug, allow your kid to disrupt my sleep and peace of mind and hunt and fish for both of you. You can lie back and eat chocolates."

In reality, you have to come down to brass tacks. Tough times are ahead.

So once we find ourselves in a situation of our own making, or not of our own making, how fast we are able to cope with tough times is going to make the difference between coming out of a disaster safely or just waiting for the spring thaw to unearth our bodies, because we just lay down and decided to give up.

Food and Water

Apart from recognizing the immediate survival conditions and situation, and your ability to cope with them, your next instinct should be – which is the best source of food? Where can I get water? How to shelter my family in the best possible way?

Unless this disaster is in a desert area, you are going to get at least some source of water available. It is going to be natural water or rain water. So once you have determined this source of water, your next priority is going to be food.

Learning How to Eat Unexpected Food Items

Imagine it is a worst case scenario. You have been flooded out. Your house has been swept away. All your electricity lines are down. All roads out of the city have been swept away, and there is no way in which rescue teams can reach you within the next month or so due to adverse weather conditions or because they just cannot get easy access to you.

You definitely do not have access to sources of quick meals, because hey, there isn't no home around. All your cans of stored food, which you made for prepping purposes for just such a disaster are now buried under 10 feet of flood water somewhere there yonder.

Now is the time to use your hunter instinct to feed you and your family.

We are very fortunate that we have such an abundance of wildlife in the shape of animals and birds and also insects all over the world. Just a few animal species are toxic and poisonous to man. The rest of them are edible. So you need to know all about the animals, which can be tracked easily and then trapped, those which live in nests, holes, and dens and how they can be made into useful sources of food for you.

Do not go in for tracking large species like caribou and elk – especially if you are living in an area where these are prolific. Save your high-caliber ammunition – if you have weapons – for emergencies. Instead, use natural traditional traps to trap any animal which swims, flies, walks, and even crawls.

I was reading Madeleine Brent's *Golden Urchin* about a young girl brought up since childhood in the Australian outback. One day she finds a white man dying in the desert, and is amazed that he is so foolish that he is allowing himself to die when there is food all around him.

Well, the white man being a civilized white man did not know that grubs, caterpillars and other living creatures were excellent sources of protein. And because he did not know this, he was starving, while a banquet flew crawled and ran around him.

People in drought ridden areas survived by eating roots, insects, bark , leaves, and tubers. In fact, I heard about a rescue operation taking place in a particularly backward and remote area in Africa, where the food supplies sent to them through the UN consisted of tins of canned fruit, which were airdropped.

Those people collected those metal cans, weighed them, calculated the odds, and then used them as weapons to bring down surviving and potential prey. They did not know how to open them. Well, they were using any available source to get another food source, even with the paucity of stones and rocks.

I also remember reading about a snooty explorer who went exploring in the jungles of deepest Africa and was bidden to a feast by the members of a friendly tribe. He looked at the fare-meat cooked in a covering of river mud. Herbs and vegetables and tubers cooked in a covering of leaves.

He did not enjoy the feast much, because as he explained in a drawl, "I could not eat that. Why, I do not eat the food cooked in our club, ever since they introduced Continental cooking, like snails and frog legs. So you cannot expect me to eat food covered in leaves and mud, dash it, I am not a bally heathen, old boy. I have my standards. "

Whether the man survived to come back to boast about his exploits in darkest Africa in his club over a whiskey and soda is debatable. But I am sure that he went on safari with Crystal and linen and his cook, cooking food fit for this insular Sahib. He never faced disaster. He never faced starvation. And so he went around peering through his eyeglass at the native cuisine of people of other countries in a superior fashion and sneered genteelly.

You of course cannot afford to be so very very nice, when it is a question of survival. There is a healthy protein source right in front of you. But hey, you have never eaten a squirrel in your life. Well, your family is going to starve because you are so very finicky and particular, and such a dainty civilized person.

A sensible person knows that his first priority is to keep healthy. Prisoners of war talk about their hands tied behind them, and they being made to lap soup like dogs by their sadistic guards. I know about one such ex- prisoner. He said that he could not afford to get all proud and stiff-necked, because that would mean mental and physical weakness. So he bore the indignity of having his face smashed into some watery liquid or some tasteless solid thrice a day by his guard, who seem to be quite a nasty piece of work.

But this prisoner intended to stay healthy, and he did. By eating and drinking all that, for that required nourishment. He had a burning will to survive.

We are not talking about you ever finding you in such a condition. But remember you cannot afford to have any prejudices about the food you eat.

Insects as Potential Food Sources

Did you know that insects, especially grasshoppers are the best sources of protein in the world? They have 75 – 80% of protein. Compare it with beef, which has 20% of protein! But we shudder at the thought of eating insects. If we had been born 5000 years ago, we would be enjoying delicacies such as huge red ants crushed, and eaten with honey as a relish with herbs and vegetables. We would naturally avoid all those insects which stung and flew, and insects which had a pungent odor.

Witchetty grubs are wood eating larvae of moths and are a delicacy in Australia. You may consider them to be an unappetizing food source in the beginning, but they are the best source of protein. Do not eat spiders, mosquitoes, flies, ticks, as these are potential disease carriers.

The best places where you can find insects to eat are under rotting logs. You are going to get grubs, termites, ants and beetles here. Chimpanzees stick a stick into an ant hole or a termite hole. Then they pull it up, covered with ants. Nice instant snack for them. If you want to try this snack, you may want to coat the stick with something sweet like syrup or honey. After all, you have more creativity than a chimpanzee.

Materials like stones, and boards are also good nesting places for insects. Just overturn them and collect all the insect life teeming under those moist places.

Naturally, I never needed to go hunting for insects to eat in the jungle as a child, but I knew that they were relished and eaten by my friends. And I shared their meals, which included pastes and minced meats made up of ingredients which would make any supposedly civilized person shudder.

Any given meal could consist of snake meat, grubs, red ants, herbs, leaves, bark, seeds, all cooked in a covering of mud in a mud oven. And I found them delicious, because I did not know what the ingredients were. It was only when they were safely digested that I found I had been eating red ants and snakes.

So what? It was tasty and we were hungry.

Remember that any insect with a hard covering like grasshoppers and beetles are going to have parasites on them. That is why they need to be cooked. Do not eat them raw. Get rid of the barbed legs and the wings, before you put them in the fire.

Most of these insects can be eaten raw. Witchetti grubs taste like almonds and when cooked, can be as tender and delicious as chicken. Grubs normally are bland in taste, when eaten raw. So if you have herbs and salt, you are going to have a tasty and protein filled meal by grinding these sources of protein together with edible herbs and other vegetation.

Catching Grasshoppers

Believe it or not, grasshoppers as an edible delicious dish are slowly and steadily catching on in the world, even though there were traditional gourmet fare in Uganda and Mexico down the ages. In fact, many people are considering this insect as a valuable source of protein in the 21st century, and ideas are being put forward that they should be harvested as a future source of food to prevent people from starving.

Catching grasshoppers is very easy. They are best caught in the morning time, when they are just waking up and are sluggish. Use the net to catch them, or if you are fast enough, catch them in your hands.

You can also try trapping them. Make a hole in a grassy place and place a jar in it. Place some bait in the shape of fruit like carrots or some green like wheat or oats in the jar. You can skip the jar on its side, so that the grasshoppers can crawl in. Leave it there overnight. In the morning you are going to find some crickets and grasshoppers in the jar. Now just place a lid with some holes over the jar and there, you are going to have your grasshoppers alive in their farm, ready for harvesting.

You can also immobilize grasshoppers while you are trapping it. Just flick a green willow wand which is about 2 ½ – 3 feet in length on a grasshopper, to hold it down in place until you can reach it. Put it in your bottle.

Grasshoppers should never be eaten raw, because they are going to carry parasites. Wings and legs should be moved before cooking. Some people just pull off the head of the grasshopper, which helps remove the internal organs. That reduces the chances of parasitic infection, because the stomach is removed. You can try that. Insert a stick or skewer through the cavity and sheesh kebab your grasshoppers over a fire.

Grasshoppers need to be cleaned before eating. So remember to wash them and dry them.

Earthworms

If you can feed fish earthworms as bait, and then eat those fish, what is to stop you from eating this excellent protein source?

Earthworms are going to be omnipresent, especially in wet ground after rain. You can also find them in rich humus laden soil. Put them in a bottle of clean water for about 10 minutes, so that they are washed properly and they purge themselves of all their waste. They are now ready for eating. You can eat them raw.

Snakes

The moment we hear the words "snakes", we feel a subconscious frisson of revulsion. That is because genetically we have been brought up to be terrified by snakes. Our anthropoidal and Simian ancestors knew snakes to be their greatest enemies, because both species considered trees to be their sole territory. That is why confronting a snake meant fighting tooth and nail for your territory, which could be taken over by a snake family.

More than 10,000 years later, we are doing the same thing with snakes trying to take over our gardens and even entering our houses, especially in the rainy season in the East.

However, we still treat snakes with respect, because we do not know much about them. According to us, all snakes are poisonous. That is not true.

Only 600 species, which is just a quarter of all the snake species all over the world are poisonous.

You may want to know more about poisonous snakes on this URL.

http://en.wikipedia.org/wiki/Venomous_snake

In many parts of Asia, snakes are considered to be a good source of food. In fact, it tastes just like soft chicken.

Once you get over the mental fear of a snake, it is just another reptile, which is going to be your food source. I remember being rather wary of snakes, as a child, because most of the feminine adults around me went into hysterical fits, whenever they saw a snake. And this was very often, especially as we lived in a jungle and in a mountainous region. For them, every snake, including pythons, and the grass snake was poisonous, and was capable of killing any living thing, human or animal.

Pythons which belonged to the boa constrictor family are not poisonous, but they are capable of swallowing their prey whole, after it has been crushed in their powerful coils.

It was only when we were in class VI, under the tutelage of a very intelligent, popular and progressive science teacher – Dr. V. G. Tikekar – that we learned that snakes were not slimy, creepy, and terrifying.

He told us that we lived in jungles, so we needed to learn about animal life. And he put his hand inside a bag and got out a real-life *grass snake.* All of us shuddered. Here was our teacher, very much admired, and he was handling snakes as if they were his best friends.

And he was taking that little snake around, and asking us to hold him. What was the matter with him? Who went around holding snakes just for fun?

Suddenly he stood in front of me and said, "Okay, you are the first of all the mischief makers and daredevils in this class. Hold it. Go ahead." I looked around. All my classmates were grinning, so glad to see me in a tough spot. That should larn me, should not it. Toughie that I was. And taking a deep breath, heart beating 19 to the dozen, I took the snake from his hands.

No, a snake is not scaly or slimy. In fact, the skin is remarkably smooth. And I noticed the snake encircling my wrist with its tail in interlocking grip. Dr. T lifted up my arm and showed the grip to everybody. "This is how the snake holds onto a branch, while it moves its body over trees."

I was so thrilled with my grass snake friend, that I became quite possessive about it, and often used to go into the vivarium, and take it out just for fun. Needless to say, it was used to terrify a couple of other classmates – male and female, who still shrank away from snakes. Once a meanie, always a meanie, especially with a harmless but scary weapon like Greenie.

Dr. T. also taught us the best way of catching a snake. He told us that once we had its head trapped, we just needed to lift it up by its tail and *whip it* through the air. That would dislocate its spinal cord. After that it was rendered harmless, and it could then be skinned, chopped up and eaten.

Naturally, people who have not confronted snakes are going to find this procedure terrifying. You need a very strong state of mind to do a thing like that, because you are always going to be afraid of the snake. Another snake tale coming up later, telling you how to manage to trap a snake, especially a cobra.

Believe it or not, all of us fell for the charms of Greenie, and we wanted grass snakes as pets, an idea formally and firmly vetoed by our scaredy-cat parents. And that is how we learned that snakes were definitely not all of them dangerous, except cobras, vipers and Kraits, which unfortunately are very common in the Indian subcontinent.

Rattlesnakes are poisonous snakes, commonly present in the USA. Mambas and other snakes are responsible for many deaths in the East and in Africa. Many times, a person may find himself bitten by an ordinary snake, protecting itself, and he dies of fright. That is because the snake has been the victim of great tall tales, down the ages. In fact, it is worshiped in the East, and there are still places in the Indian subcontinent and Africa, where killing a snake is taboo. That is because there is a myth that its partner is going to search you out and take revenge for its mate.

Well, whether this is true or not, here is the second snake – cobra – tale – which is part of family history recounted to us kids by our father – because it stars me at crawling on all fours stage, eight hens, one spaniel, one set of parents, one angry cobra and one bamboo stick.

This drama began when this huge poisonous hooded cobra got cornered in the yard by the hens. So it immediately spread its hood and started to sway. The hens made a semicircle around it, looking for the chance to strike. Humans are under the impression that birds are normally petrified when they are confronted with snakes, but these particular White Leghorns had not heard that rule. I got into the act by crawling into the vicinity, and the protective spaniel following me came, saw and set up a yelp.

Mother was in the kitchen, father was in the bathroom. Hearing such a noise, both of them came out and of course mom nearly went into shock. There was her little baby, crawling right towards the cobra, ready to grasp it. [I did not seem to have any sense of self-preservation, since babyhood, it seems.]

Father immediately asked mom to call the dog back. The dog was not coming back, no not he, as long as he saw me in a danger zone. Mom acted with dad in instinctive synchronicity. She dived for her baby, and distracted the cobra enough for dad to get hold of the bamboo. This was about 6 feet long, and with an arms length of 2 feet, the cobra could not strike father.

As she took me to the safety of the kitchen, with a very thankful spaniel following her, Dad began swaying the bamboo stick, in a scything movement sideways in front of the cobra and above its hood. He was lucky that he had plenty of space to swing that flexible bamboo in the air. This may not be possible in a restricted place.

An iron Rod is definitely not going to do. Firstly, it is too heavy. Secondly, it is not so flexible. Thirdly, it does not have the give of a bamboo stick or a long thick willow whip.

What is with the swaying of the stick?

He was just emulating that old Indian cliché, the snake charmer. The cobra is not dancing to the tune of the musical instrument. Snakes are deaf. A dancing cobra is actually just moving from side to side, looking for the right place to strike. The snake charmer also moves his body rhythmically at the same time. A static snake charmer is just asking to be bitten.

That was what the rod was doing. Do not try to hit the hooded cobra with one supposedly effective blow on the hood. You are not going to be very certain of connecting with the hood, in the very first blow, especially when you are standing 8 feet away.

Anyway, 1 swing and the now distracted cobra put its head down. That was that. It was immediately pinned down the next second. And then dispatched with repeated quick blows to head and spinal cord.

We lived in that house for the next three years and there was definitely no revenge seeking mate of that particular cobra ravening for the blood of the human inhabitants. The birds got out of the way, when they saw dad getting into the act. They dined off chopped headless cobra mixed with their fish meal for the next week and they were none the worse.

So your survival kit must have one really light, flexible long and sturdy bamboo shoot or willow whip, which is not only a survival weapon, but also a thing to protect you.

Other Reptiles and Amphibians

These cold-blooded reptiles are an excellent source of protein. They are best eaten cooked, which is going to kill all the parasites. Eat them raw, only during an emergency.

Box turtles are reptiles which you are not going to eat, raw or cooked. That is because it can digest poisonous mushrooms, while you cannot. If you are in the Atlantic Ocean, and find yourself face to face with the hawksbill turtle, do not eat it. It has a poisonous thorax. Large sea turtles should be avoided.

Box turtle

This is what survivor trainers say, but on the other hand, other people live off turtle meat and consider it to be quite a delicacy. I would say that if you chop way off its head and neck, thus effectively removing the thorax region, the rest of the turtle is going to be edible, *nicht war*?

Living off Crustaceans

Shrimps, crayfish, Marine lobsters, crabs and prawns are excellent sources of food. These can easily be collected during the day by looking under stones in water sources. Crayfish can easily be caught by putting strings on which you have knotted pieces of meat in the water source. The moment the crayfish grabs a piece of meat, just haul it out before it releases the bait.

How to Make a Shrimping/Fishing Net

I made a really effective shrimping net by using a fine meshed old butterfly net. I pushed its handle into a hollow and light curtain rod. Not only did that give me more length, when I sat on the pier and fished for shrimp at low tide, but I did not have to go to sea on a boat like the owl and the pussycat.

I found this URL rather interesting which shows you how to make nets your own self. Interesting DIY project. The aaa seems to be part of his teaching technique while he is getting his thoughts together, but even so, the process was remarkably effective.

https://www.youtube.com/watch?v=sRJLAac86hg

It was only after I finished seeing it, that the light switched on in my head. What he was doing was known to arty crafty women kind as macramé network! I needed to watch the whole video, saying to myself, this procedure looks familiar, this procedure looks familiar. Till the mental tube light switched on.

You may want to buy the net from the market, but it is more interesting making your own net . If you have 4-5 hours free like the guide on that particular URL.

There is some information on shrimping Nets.

http://shrimpin.com/nets.htm

Shrimps along with crabs and lobsters are attracted to light at night, so you can scoop them up with a shrimping net. You can also put out bait to entice crabs and lobsters.

This URL is also interesting.

http://www.ehow.com/how_5511006_build-shrimp-trap-catch-shrimp.html?ref=Track2&utm_source=ask

Fish

You are never going to starve if you have a water source with fish. Freshwater fish are excellent sources of protein and nutrition as well as fat. The positive thing about fish is that they are more abundant life forms, than other mammals and reptiles and easier to catch, especially if you know their habits.

Fish are going to feed heavily on the surface before a storm. So get your fishing net out and cast it upon the waters. They are not going to feed after the storm because at that time, the water is muddy.

If the flowing water has a current, try fishing in areas near rocks, where the water eddies or is comparatively still.

My favorite fisherman writer – Maurice Walsh -often talked about some legendary local fish in his stories, which has evaded fishermen for years. Everybody knows that it lives or rests under a rock and let the flowing river pass him by. Also, fishes, gather together under brush which is overhanging, pools, which are deep, foliage, which is submerged – excellent and protective camouflage around and in that foliage and other places which can offer them shelter, like rocks and logs.

Also fishes are attracted to light at night, and that is why they come up to the surface, if they see lights shining. That is why night fishing is so popular in many parts of the world.

Freshwater fish are definitely not poisonous. I did not eat catfish for ever so long, because one of my friends told me a fishy tale that it was inedible. Till one day I caught her dining off fresh catfish with corn and Okra-a traditional family Creole dish. When I snarled that she had been pulling my leg and I was thankful I did not write about this particular fishes' toxicity in my survival books, she gave me a really smarmy grin and told me that I was so gullible. I believed everything, especially when it is told to mean a very serious wide-eyed tone.

Catfish are dangerous only to the point that the protrusions present on their barbels and which are also present on the dorsal fins are capable of puncturing your skin, and these may get infected.

Freshwater fish are definitely not eaten raw. You need to cook them to get rid of any parasites. Somehow, you do not have to worry about parasites in Marine fish, because the salt water content kills off any parasites. That is why shipwrecked sailors who could not build fires subsisted off raw fish caught from the sea. And they stayed healthy.

Poisonous fish species include puffer fish, red snapper, globefish, Sunfish thorn fish, cow fish, Jack, balloon fish and porcupine fish. That is because they have a poisonous toxin-tetrodotoxin which causes immediate paralysis and death. Barracudas are not poisonous, but if they are eaten raw, they can cause toxic poisoning.

About five years ago, eating puffer fish became a fad by gourmets, who were literally dicing with death, if they ate Fugu. In fact, I remember reading a Haiku , which says

I cannot see her tonight.
I have to give her up
So I will eat fugu.

So he could not care less whether he lives or dies, that is why he does not mind about he being poisoned through blowfish liver. By the way, Japanese consider this dish to be an expensive gourmet fare, especially when it has been made by a trained cook. Westerners are more cautious, because they may have tried it out in some restaurant with untrained cooks and that is why a fatality was assured.

Fugu- blow fish

Do not try out fugu when you are out trying to survive. Call it stupidity, taking chances, foolhardiness, or suicide – when it is a question of survival, why are you looking for the easiest way to die?

Making Fish Traps

https://www.youtube.com/watch?v=ACAAb0SZjtU

This URL is rather complex for beginners, but it gives you a lot of information. Especially the cutting bamboo shoots with a knife part. Not to be done by an amateur. There are also some extremely interesting tips, like making knots and using huge plastic bottles for trapping fish. The about one is good for tips, the one below is much more comprehensive, especially when you learn how to make an inner trap. The URL given below has a more easy weaving technique and I am going to make a basket in an afternoon.

Next time I try making vine baskets and traps, I will know how to make them, without cutting my hands on bamboo strips.

http://beforeitsnews.com/survival/2013/12/survival-fishing-how-to-make-a-primitive-basket-fish-trap-2504034.html

Remember that the spokes need to be **ODD** in number so that the weaving cord can go over, under, over, under , and so on between the vines.

This is how the professionals do it-especially when they go fishing on trawlers.

http://www.wikihow.com/Make-a-Fish-Trap

Also, this is an easy DIY.

http://www.instructables.com/id/Building-A-Cheap-Fish-Trap-DIY-For-catching-fish/

The fishing bait, which he said was white bread is an excellent choice. Believe it or not, I found that a little bit of asafoetida powder added to that of white bread entices fish even more. Wonder why, because I consider that spice highly smelly in its raw form, though tasty in its cooked form. Try that out.

Collecting Mollusks

The Mollusks Class are just not restricted to shellfish, they are also going to include mussels, snails, octopuses, periwinkles, clams and other bivalves.

So okay, popular literature shows octopuses to be really dangerous and popular colloquialisms have the local wolves described as having more hands than an octopus. Octopus meat is a delicacy, and how do octopus fishermen use the traditional method to catch them in the East? Well, they just dive down into the sea, and look around for octopuses. After that, when they find one, they go near it, and *bite the fleshy area between its eyes.*

I am definitely not so brave as to do that, so the next time I meet an octopus underwater, I am just going to stick my friendly neighborhood knife in between that area between its eyes-its brains. I would rather sink my teeth in cooked octopus, than an energetic octopus on its own home ground.

Funnily enough, the British enjoy eating whelks, Periwinkles and cockles, especially in seaside resorts like Rocksalt and Folkestone, but they do not want to eat snails – aquatic or the garden-variety. They do not know that periwinkles are sea snails The Welsh enjoy a cockle breakfast with bacon and bread, but a Frenchman is always called a frog and snail eater by their neighbors!

Also, abalones and oysters are considered to be a delicacy, because there are so expensive. On the other hand whelks, winkles and cockles were once eaten on the seashores of Kent, fresh off the fishing boats, with salt sprinkled on them and the meat removed with toothpicks lost popularity in the 19 century, because they were "common fare".

Cockles

You can eat them today, by picking out the meat with a tooth pick and dipping it in butter, or sauce, just for fun, if you are trying out foodstuffs which are edible. In the same way, you can cook whelks, with their shells still on in a stirfry. They are not going to look really good, but they are tasty, nutritious and filled with protein.

These periwinkles and other shellfish are easily available in lakes, streams and rivers. Common mollusks are found in still or flowing fresh water, with muddy or sandy bottoms. You can recognize their trail, which they leave while passing in the mud. You can also look for them, by searching for dark and elliptical slits of open valves.

Shellfish, limpets and snails can also be found clinging to rocks near wet sand and tidal pools. Always remember to collect seaweed coming in from the sea. You are going to get a rich store of animal life clinging to it, including fish and mollusks. Chitons , or large snails can be found on a rock surface above a surf line.

Mussels like oysters, are going to be found in mussel beds and colonies. You can look for them near Boulder bases, on top of logs and in rocky pools.

Oysters are eaten raw, but personally, I thought them tasting a bit like chewing on rubber. The little bit of lemon juice and salt improved the taste, but like I said, it is an acquired taste.

These mollusks are excellent with tubers, greens and steamed, boiled and baked in their shells.

Precautions –

If you are living in a tropical area, do not eat mussels in the summer. They are toxic, then. Also, any shellfish which have not been covered with water during high tide should not be collected and added to your mollusk collection. They definitely are not fit to be eaten. Same idea of toxicity. Underwater mollusks are safe to eat. Those on the surface to which the high tide does not reach should be avoided.

Collecting Amphibians

Salamanders and frogs are good eating. Remember to avoid all those frogs which are colored brightly. Any frog with an X sign on its back is telling you to keep away. Toads are poisonous. Learn how to recognize the difference between a toad and a frog.

Frogs prefer a wet environment near the water, or its edge. Toads can be found far away from water. The skin of a toad is toxic and more Warty. It is also going to secrete poisons. So do not go around handing toads and do not eat them.

Frog meat, especially roasted over fire with salamander meat is good protein. Just go out near water sources at night with a light. You can search them out near mud banks and Rocky places in the water.

Eating birds

Birds have been part of human cuisine for millenniums, so you may be used to eating birds. All of them are edible, but some may have flesh flavors which are oily, gamy and strong, especially if they are species which eat fish.

The flavor of Gulls and albatrosses can be made milder, if you remove the skin, along with the feathers.

Roosting birds can be removed by hand at night from their perches. Many birds do not move from their nests, especially during nesting season and you can thus capture them. Once you know where they are nesting, catch them at night.

Birds move over one particular path while going to their feeding place, and coming back to their nest.

I wrote about this in my book – the wonderful world of birds-

http://www.amazon.com/Wonderful-World-Birds-Friends-Feathered-ebook/dp/B00H59YE5G/ref=sr_1_5?s=digital-text&ie=UTF8&qid=1400268240&sr=1-5&keywords=john+davidson+birds

Once we know all about the path taken by birds, it is very easy to set out traps in those areas. Just stretch out bird nets. You can also place these nets near water sources or near roosting areas to trap these birds when they come back to their trees at dusk.

Here is one tip on how you can get a regular source of birds eggs from a birds nest. Look for a birds nest, when the bird is away. Just leave four – five eggs in the clutch, and mark them so that they are easily recognizable. Remove the rest and enjoy fried, boiled or raw bird eggs. The bird is going to lay more eggs to fill up her nest. Remove these fresh eggs after four days, while allowing the marked eggs to hatch.

The bird brain cannot count. So she will be happy with her four – five chicks.

Mammals as a food source

Mammals are excellent food sources. The only problem with them is that they are difficult to trap, especially when they are large in size. Also, they are capable of biting. I remember an interesting episode in the life and times of world-famous naturalist Gerald Durrell. When asked how he had received a particularly nasty looking scar. He left the audience with an impression that it was a pleasant altercation with a leopard. He did not want to tell them that an angry little squirrel had taken out a chunk of his anatomy. After all, squirrels, like chipmunks were so cute, and how could they bite?

Let me tell you this sad, sad hilarious tale in the life and times of yours truly. Now being an avid fan of Gerald Durrell, and a bit of a naturalist myself, here I was at college, trying to make friends with squirrels. I wanted one as a pet, and there was this really cute little itsy-bitsy baby, which I had managed to Lull into a feeling of false security by feeding it biscuits on my windowsill.

This went on for a week. One fine morning, before classes started, I decided that I was going to catch my baby squirrel, and take it to class. I would have the only squirrel in college.

So the moment Li'l Sqill'ell came around, sniffing for biscuits, I handed it one, and when it was near me, I pounced. And grabbed it. I still wonder who was more surprised, I with my handful of agitated baby squirrel or it finding it in my fist.

It immediately swung into action by sinking its teeth into the back of my thumb.

Now I had this crazy idea, which I had read somewhere that you need to press the tummy of an animal in order to make it let go. So I pressed its tummy, shouting "Leggo you" or squeaking all the while, as blood flew copiously. It definitely was not going to let go- it had decided that as it sank its teeth to the bone and held on for dear life. Anybody who pressed its tummy deserved everything coming to her.

So what could I do? I ran still squeaking down the college corridor, – incidentally, leaving a trail of blood all the way – to my zoology professor, – Major A.M, who was a retired and trained army officer. She would know how to save me from this dangerous little animal.

Her immediate reaction was, "let it go"! My answer was, "I am trying to, but it does not want to let go." And we just stood there helplessly while I kept losing all that blood.

Anyway, after a little while, the squirrel suddenly found that my palms were open and away it ran. My college professors who already considered me a bit of a clown, wanted to know how I had caught it while Major. Mathur washed and bandaged my battle wound. I told them that I had just pounced on it and caught it.

I could see it in their eyes an unasked question, "But why would you want to catch a squirrel," but being sensible ladies and gentlemen, they did not want to go into the psyche of a 17-year-old. Besides, they knew the answer they would get from me. "Because it was there, all ready to catch."

Elementary, my dear Watson.

However, I noticed them treating me with plenty of wariness for the rest of the academic session. Otherwise, I was normal in all other respects.

So remember that even little squirrels are dangerous. Rest of the story? It turned up the very next morning, chirping away and asking for biscuits. I threw one of my cherished flying boots at it and used rude language. It answered back in kind. Boots instead of biscuits eh? Oh no, it was not having any. It wanted its breakfast. I had a sore thumb? Well, I was to blame. Why did I go and press its little tummy? All this and more.

Well, it got its breakfast. And the worst thing is that it brought all its friends around, in the coming days, all of them asking me noisily – So, how is your thumb, oh human, and yep, we want some of those biscuits, peanuts and coconut ones for choice. So snap to it!

And I timidly said aye aye sirs and complied. These tiny little things are great tyrants and can cow down hulking huge human bullies, especially those with unlimited sources of goodies.

And yes, I still have the scar of that wound on my thumb.

So remember that these food sources are excellent eating, especially when roasted-on fires. So next time you are in the woods, try hares, rabbits and other small sources of food. Position them near sources of water or on paths, which these animals frequent.

Please look at this URL

https://www.youtube.com/watch?v=jKJHxORY7Tw

Conclusion

I hope you liked this volume of our disasters series, telling you more about survival and food sources. You may want to use this information just for general use, and try some basket making, as an interesting hobby. The more skills you have, the more chances you have of survival.

Live long and prosper. And learn how to survive

Author Bio

Dueep Jyot Singh is a Management and IT Professional who managed to gather Postgraduate qualifications in Management and English and Degrees in Science, French and Education while pursuing different enjoyable career options like being an hospital administrator, IT,SEO and HRD Database Manager/ trainer, movie , radio and TV scriptwriter, theatre artiste and public speaker, lecturer in French, Marketing and Advertising, ex-Editor of Hearts On Fire (now known as Solstice) Books Missouri USA, advice columnist and cartoonist, publisher and Aviation School trainer, ex-moderator on Medico.in, banker, student councilor ,travelogue writer … among other things!

One fine morning, she decided that she had enough of killing herself by Degrees and went back to her first love -- writing. It's more enjoyable! She already has 48 published academic and 14 fiction- in- different- genre books under her belt.

When she is not designing websites or making Graphic design illustrations for clients , she is browsing through old bookshops hunting for treasures, of which she has an enviable collection – including R.L. Stevenson, O.Henry, Dornford Yates, Maurice Walsh, De Maupassant, Victor Hugo, Sapper, C.N. Williamson, "Bartimeus" and the crown of her collection- Dickens "The Old Curiosity Shop," and so on… Just call her "Renaissance Woman" - collecting herbal remedies, acting like Universal Helping Hand/Agony Aunt, or escaping to her dear mountains for a bit of exploring, collecting herbs and plants, and trekking.

Check out some of the other JD-Biz Publishing books

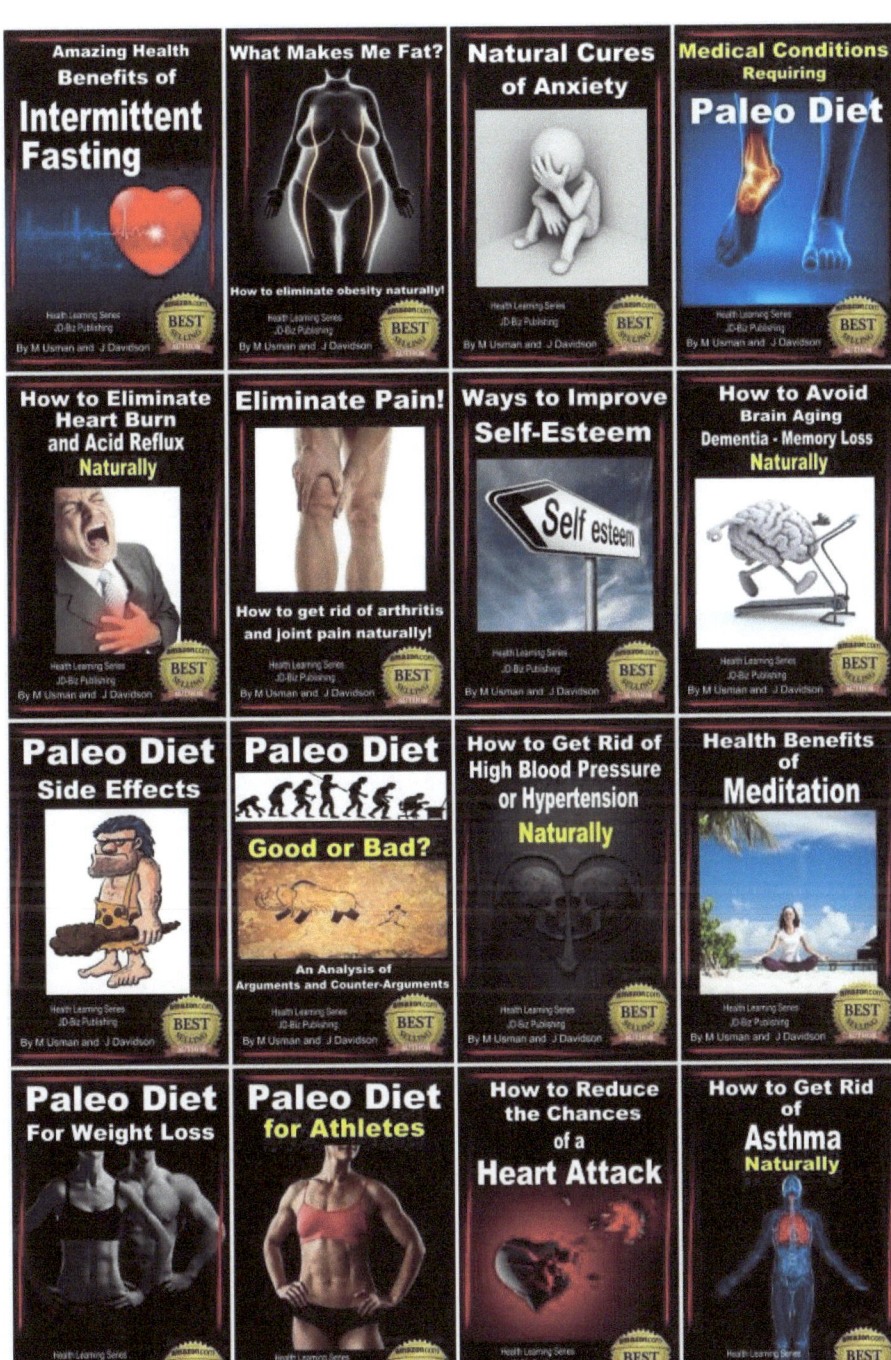

Learn To Draw Series

How to Build and Plan Books

Entrepreneur Book Series

Our books are available at

1. Amazon.com

2. Barnes and Noble

3. Itunes

4. Kobo

5. Smashwords

6. Google Play Books

Download Free Books!

http://MendonCottageBooks.com

Publisher

JD-Biz Corp

P O Box 374

Mendon, Utah 84325

http://www.jd-biz.com/